MW00353436

IMAGES
of America

THE QUADRANGLE

The Quadrangle and its iconic clock tower, seen in this 1890s photograph, have come to symbolize Fort Sam Houston just as the Alamo symbolizes San Antonio. Built as a quartermaster supply depot in 1876, the building was adapted to changing military requirements and was designated a National Historic Landmark in 1974. (Fort Sam Houston Museum.)

ON THE COVER: Taken shortly after the installation of the clock in 1882, this image shows the courtyard within the Quadrangle. The meticulously landscaped grounds and water features give no hint that this is one of the most important military headquarters and logistical facilities in the United States. With minimal physical changes, the Quadrangle remains one of the most important military installations in the country. (Fort Sam Houston Museum.)

IMAGES
of America

THE QUADRANGLE

John M. Manguso

ARCADIA
PUBLISHING

Published by Arcadia Publishing
Charleston, South Carolina

Printed in the United States of America

Library of Congress Control Number: 2017958321

For all general information, please contact Arcadia Publishing:
Telephone 843-853-2070
Fax 843-853-0044
E-mail sales@arcadiapublishing.com
For customer service and orders:
Toll-Free 1-888-313-2665

Visit us on the Internet at www.arcadiapublishing.com

This book is dedicated to my father, Angelo Manguso, who made sure I got "good marks" in school. Well, Spike, it paid off!

CONTENTS

Acknowledgments   6

Introduction   7

1.   The Quartermaster Depot on Government Hill   11

2.   The Central Point   27

3.   A Hub of Military Activity   53

4.   National Historic Landmark   77

5.   The Quadrangle in the 21st Century   107

6.   How to Date the Quadrangle Images   119

About the Organization   127

ACKNOWLEDGMENTS

The majority of images in this volume appear courtesy of the Fort Sam Houston Museum (FSHM). For their help in providing the images in this book, I thank Martin Callahan, formerly of the Fort Sam Houston Museum; the Library of Congress (LOC); the Historic American Buildings Survey (HABS); and the Defense Video and Imagery Distribution System (DVIDS). Thanks also go to the US Army's Office of the Chief of Public Affairs–Northeast and the Public Affairs Office at Army North (Fifth Army) in the Quadrangle.

I would also like to thank Ruth Dunmire, my first history teacher, for getting me interested in history; Dr. John K. Mahon, my advisor in graduate school at the University of Florida; Brig. Gen. Joseph P. Kingston, who gave me my job as military history detachment commander; Maj. Gen. Henry Mohr, chief of the Army Reserve, who advised me to "tell it like it is, even if no one believes you"; Maj. Bennie Boles, who hired me as a museum curator at Fort Sam Houston; Col. Jim O'Neal, Ed Miller, and Ron Still, three of the best supervisors a museum director could have; Joan Gaither, whose support as president of Preservation Fort Sam Houston has been invaluable; and Caroline Anderson, my title manager at Arcadia Publishing, who provided support and guidance throughout the preparation of this book. Special thanks go to Jacqueline Davis, who was my strong right arm for most of my 33 years at the Fort Sam Houston Museum. Most of all, I thank my beloved wife of 51 years, Barbara, whose support has been and continues to be priceless.

INTRODUCTION

The image that comes to mind when people talk about Fort Sam Houston is the Quadrangle with its iconic clock tower. The Quadrangle can be seen in the paintings of Porfirio Salinas and Elias San Miguel and in the jewelry of James Avery. Among historic structures in Texas, the Quadrangle is surpassed only by the Alamo, the "Cradle of Texas Liberty," in historical significance. Listed in the National Register of Historic Places, the Quadrangle looks more like a park than a military headquarters as deer and peacocks roam the grounds. On the contrary, the Quadrangle is an active participant in national defense. For almost a century and a half, the Quadrangle has been a hub of military activity.

When the US Army came to San Antonio in 1845, facilities in town included a supply depot, a small garrison, and, after the Mexican War, a regional headquarters—all located in buildings leased by the Army. The San Antonio Quartermaster Depot occupied the grounds of the Alamo. Under the Treaty of Guadalupe Hidalgo of 1848, the Rio Grande became the southern border of Texas, and Mexico ceded the land that would become Arizona, New Mexico, Colorado, Utah, Nevada, and California. The 8th Military Department, established in August 1848, moved to San Antonio in December. Before the Civil War, the Army in Texas fought 84 engagements against hostile Indians. In February 1861, secessionist Texas troops seized the depot and forced the surrender of the garrison and headquarters. Following the end of the hostilities, federal troops returned.

Concerned with the cost of the Post at San Antonio, the Army considered moving the depot and headquarters. The city council made several offers of land to keep the Army in town, and the Army accepted three parcels of land totaling 93 acres northeast of downtown. This site was called Government Hill. On May 10, 1875, construction of a depot was authorized.

On June 7, 1876, the government contracted with Edward Braden and Company to build the depot for $83,900. Work began two weeks later. Capt. George W. Davis, constructing quartermaster, reported on February 4, 1878, that work on the depot was complete. Construction had cost just under $100,000. The building measured 624 feet on each side. On the south side were 12 ground-floor rooms with a 16-foot-wide arched sally port with a stairwell leading upstairs to 12 quartermaster offices. The two wings of the building were single-story and contained 14 storerooms each. The west wing was used for storing grain; the east, for flour.

The buildings aggregated 48,600 square feet of storage space and 12,500 square feet of office space. Each storeroom had an arched entry with a divided door opening onto the courtyard. On the north side was a 24-foot-high wall with wagon sheds and shops for blacksmiths and wheelwrights. Beyond were corrals, hay yards, and woodyards.

On July 9, 1878, work began on extending the second story the full length of the building, adding office space for the headquarters. This was completed on November 4, but the headquarters would not move until 1881 when quarters were built west of the depot. At that point, all the military activities in San Antonio were located on Government Hill except the San Antonio Arsenal, which had been established in 1855.

In 1884, Congress allocated funds for the construction of a large, permanent post near the depot. Of San Antonio's location, good rail network, and water supply, Lt. Gen. William Tecumseh Sherman noted that "everything conspires to the conclusion that San Antonio must become the central point from which troops can and will radiate to the Rio Grande frontier from Fort Brown up to the mouth of the Pecos—500 miles."

Barracks and quarters were built east of the Quadrangle. Except for operations against the Apaches in 1885 and 1886, the department headquarters and the depot conducted "normal peacetime duties," a routine of drill, inspections, and reviews, with occasional field exercises as supplies were received and distributed throughout the department. This routine was interrupted in September 1886 when the Apache war chief Geronimo was brought to the Quadrangle while Pres. Grover Cleveland considered treating him as a prisoner of war or turning him over to state authorities. After six weeks, Geronimo was sent to Florida as a prisoner of war. In September 1890, the War Department issued General Order No. 99 designating the Post at San Antonio as Fort Sam Houston. In its 45th year of existence, the post finally had a proper name.

After the battleship USS *Maine* blew up in Havana Harbor on February 15, 1898, the depot began issuing supplies and equipment as garrison units prepared for service in Cuba, Puerto Rico, and the Philippines. The 1st US Volunteer Cavalry Regiment assembled in San Antonio in May at the International Fairgrounds. Equipment for these "Rough Riders" was issued by the depot. They would charge up San Juan Hill (actually Kettle Hill) in Cuba, propelling Lt. Col. Theodore Roosevelt into the White House. The war with Spain led to an expansion of the Army, which in turn led to the expansion of Fort Sam Houston into a brigade post. At the same time, the staff of the headquarters was growing. To accommodate that growth, some storerooms were converted to offices.

Revolution in Mexico in 1910 led to turmoil along the border. In 1911, the president ordered the mobilization of the Maneuver Division at Fort Sam Houston. Following this exercise, the Army began to reinforce the border. In 1913, the Department of Texas was superseded by the Southern Department, which included the states of Texas, Arkansas, Oklahoma, New Mexico, and Arizona. The focus for the Southern Department was the border with Mexico, stretching from Brownsville, Texas, to the California state line. The Quadrangle became a general depot, handling all types of supplies. Storage space was down to about 15,000 square feet, about one quarter of the total space. The remainder of the Quadrangle was used for staff offices. Storage space for the rest of the supplies required by the Southern Department was located elsewhere on post and in rented buildings in the city.

Pancho Villa's raid on Columbus, New Mexico, on March 9, 1916, led to the dispatch of the Punitive Expedition under Brig. Gen. John J. Pershing. This force was directed by Gen. Frederick Funston's headquarters in the Quadrangle and supported by the depot. To secure the border area, President Wilson called out the National Guard. By early 1917, the Southern Department was the largest command in the United States.

When the United States declared war on Germany in April 1917, the Army rapidly expanded to some four million men in uniform. The Southern Department and the depot both played major roles in the war effort. Six mobilization cantonments in the Southern Department were established, with four in Texas. Additional posts, camps, and stations were established, including a host of Air Service facilities. The Southern Department headquarters managed and supported these installations, the associated mobilization and deployment machinery, and the US Border Patrol.

The San Antonio General Depot employed 3,030 civilians and 363 officers and enlisted men. Another 1,726 civilians conducted reclamation and salvage operations. The depot had almost 600,000 square feet of rented storage space in San Antonio and 300,000 square feet at Fort Sam Houston, Kelly Field, and other military installations. During the war, the San Antonio General Depot supplied 42 posts, camps, and stations in Texas; four installations in New Mexico; five in Arizona; four in Oklahoma; and one each in Arkansas and Louisiana. By this time, it had become apparent that both the depot and the headquarters could no longer fit in the Quadrangle. In 1917, the War Department purchased land northeast of the Quadrangle for a new depot. Construction began in 1920. When the new depot opened in 1921, the headquarters was the sole occupant of the Quadrangle.

After the armistice in November 1918, the Southern Department headquarters and depot were involved in demobilizing the Army and disposing of surplus materiel and real estate. Congress passed the National Defense Act of 1920, which established the new Corps Areas. The Southern Department became the VIII Corps Area, comprising the states of Texas, Oklahoma, New Mexico, Arizona, and Colorado. This headquarters was responsible for administration of units and installations within its area and for training the Regular Army, National Guard, and Organized Reserve units. The act also established a Third Army headquarters, command of which rotated between the commanders of the IV and VIII Corps Areas.

As the country suffered through the Great Depression, the VIII Corps Area supported the Civilian Conservation Corps (CCC) districts within Texas, Oklahoma, New Mexico, Colorado, and Louisiana. There would be 42 CCC companies in Texas, aggregating 10,170 men. CCC activities occupied nine rooms in the Quadrangle.

In 1933, the Third Army headquarters was activated at Fort Sam Houston as a tactical element and moved to Atlanta in 1936. It would return in 1940 and occupy space in the Smith-Young Tower in San Antonio. After the German invasion of Poland in 1939, President Roosevelt authorized the expansion of the Army and the National Guard. In May 1940, the Army resumed large-scale maneuvers in the VIII Corps Area. The Selective Training & Service Act of September 16, 1940, was passed. In September 1940, mobilization of the National Guard divisions began.

Following the attack on Pearl Harbor, the Army was organized into the Army Ground Forces, the Services of Supply (soon changed to the Army Service Forces), and the Army Air Forces. The Third Army was part of the Army Ground Forces; the VIII Corps Area, redesignated as the VIII Service Command, became part of the Army Service Forces and moved to Dallas, Texas. The Third Army headquarters then moved into the Quadrangle.

In January 1943, the Sixth Army headquarters was formed with personnel drawn from the Third Army and deployed to the Pacific theater. In January 1944, the Third Army went overseas, and the Fourth Army in California moved into the Quadrangle. The Fourth Army headquarters then provided cadres to form the Ninth, Tenth, and Fifteenth Armies, which deployed overseas. In addition to producing field Army headquarters, the headquarters in the Quadrangle supervised the organization, training, and deployment of units of all types. In February 1945, the War Department assigned the Fourth Army the mission of training units returning from Europe for employment in the Pacific theater and redeploying them to that theater. The end of the war changed that mission to one of receiving and processing soldiers back to civilian life.

During the war, the headquarters of the Fourth Army shipped almost half of all of the divisions that served overseas. In the last 12 months of the war alone, the Fourth Army shipped 16 divisions and another 571 units, totaling 354,000 soldiers. Following the war, the Army determined that the facilities at Fort Sam Houston and Camp Bullis were insufficient for a combat division but the headquarters mission performed in the Quadrangle would remain. Medical training activities were transferred here, beginning with the Medical Field Service School. The post became the "home of Army Medicine."

On May 14, 1946, the Fourth Army area included the states of Texas, Arkansas, Louisiana, Oklahoma, and New Mexico, and all units, posts, camps, stations, and installations within this area except those of the Army Air Forces, destined to become a separate service in 1947. Fourth Army was responsible for operations, training, administrative services, and supply within this area. It also supervised and inspected the ROTC, the National Guard, and the Organized Reserve Corps.

During the Korean War, the Fourth Army mobilized four divisions for the Far East and for NATO in Europe and 83 other Reserve Component units as part of the overall military buildup. Cold War deployments continued into the 1960s, including the Berlin and the Cuban Missile Crises. During the communist insurgency in South Vietnam, Fourth Army headquarters deployed 313 units of all sizes, totaling 46,000 troops, to Vietnam.

On June 30 1971, the Fourth and Fifth Army areas were combined into a single, 13-state area, and the Fourth Army was inactivated. The Fifth Army headquarters moved from Chicago into the Quadrangle. Under the 1972 reorganization of the Army, the Fifth Army was to focus on the training and readiness of the Reserve Component units within its area. In 1974, Fort Sam Houston was declared a National Historic Landmark and the Quadrangle was listed in the National Register of Historic Places.

During the Reagan administration, Reserve Component units in the Fifth Army area participated in major exercises within the United States and overseas, including rotations at the National Training Center and the Joint Readiness Training Center and exercises in Europe, Korea, the Middle East, and Central America. Reserve Component soldiers from the Fifth Army area also served during operations in Grenada and Panama.

During Operation Desert Shield and Operation Desert Storm, in Saudi Arabia and Kuwait in 1990 and 1991 respectively, the Fifth Army mobilized some 27,000 citizen-soldiers from more than 200 Reserve Component units. Reserve Component units also served in northern Iraq and in Somalia in 1993. During operations in Haiti, Lt. Gen. Joseph W. Kinzer, the deputy commanding general of Fifth Army, served as commander of the United Nations forces.

Emphasis on the Reserve Component units continued after the Gulf War. The motto "In Peace, Prepare for War," displayed on the tower since 1877, was reemphasized. During the tenure of Lt. Gen. Tom Jaco, renovation projects were undertaken in the Quadrangle, which reflected his concern with the National Historic Landmark status of the site. The corridor along the second story displayed the history of the Quadrangle and the headquarters. In the stairwell, a painting entitled A Heritage of Service, by Elias San Miguel and Richard Sanchez, showed the tower flanked by portraits representing the many generations of soldiers who served at Fort Sam Houston. The arcade was reopened with a double-pane insulated-glass wall in lieu of the wood siding. This restored the original appearance of the open arcade while still accommodating the air-conditioning.

In 1995, the Fifth Army headquarters consisted of about 250 assigned military personnel and civilian employees. It provided training support in a 21-state area of responsibility. In 1997, the mission of responding to weapons of mass destruction incidents was added.

Following the attacks on the World Trade Center and the Pentagon on September 11, 2001, access onto Fort Sam Houston was severely restricted. To confront ongoing security challenges, the United States created the US Northern Command (NORTHCOM) in 2002 to handle homeland defense and civil support operations. On October 1, 2005, Fifth Army headquarters began to transform into Army North/Fifth Army. In the event of a terrorist incident, natural disaster, invasion, or a chemical/biological/radiological event, the headquarters in the Quadrangle would have appropriate types of units assigned to it to meet the situation. When augmented, the headquarters could deploy as a joint task force headquarters or as a joint forces land component command. Army North/Fifth Army's area of responsibility included all of North America.

In 2005, Congress began the Base Realignment and Closure process to reconfigure the Department of Defense infrastructure and optimize it for warfighting capability and efficiency. The results signaled significant changes for Fort Sam Houston and the Quadrangle. Some 14,000 people moved to the post as Army, Navy, and Air Force activities and units were transferred there. Fort Sam Houston became part of Joint Base San Antonio under the 502nd Airbase Wing, commanded by an Air Force brigadier general. The post changed from "the Home of Army Medicine" to "the home of Military Medicine" as the Medical Education and Training Campus added Air Force and Navy enlisted medical training to the installation. The biggest change for the Quadrangle was that the Fort Sam Houston Museum joined the headquarters, occupying the east wing of the building in June 2015.

In the 142 years since it was built as the San Antonio Quartermaster Depot, the Quadrangle has played an important role in national defense. The Quadrangle has changed, both structurally and functionally, while retaining its essential architectural character. Many of America's most distinguished soldiers have served there. As its service extends farther into the 21st century, the Quadrangle will continue as a hub of military activity in Texas and beyond.

One

THE QUARTERMASTER DEPOT ON GOVERNMENT HILL

When the Army arrived in San Antonio, it established a supply depot in the Alamo. For the use of that building and the barracks, quarters, and office space it used, the Army paid rent. After the Civil War, the Army considered leaving San Antonio to avoid paying the rent. At the same time, the city council wanted the Army out of downtown because it received no tax revenue on the real estate used by the Army but it did not want to lose the economic benefits generated by the Army's presence. When asked by the city council what would keep the Army in town, the post commander replied that the Army would stay if it had a permanent post. The city then made a series of offers of land. Between 1870 and 1875, the Army accepted three parcels totaling 93 acres north of town. The city council also offered the Army the use of the city rock quarries for stone to the construct the buildings. The quarries would eventually be home to the San Antonio Zoo and the Sunken Garden Theater.

Construction began in June the following year. The constructing quartermaster, Capt. George W. Davis, hired a photographer to record the construction. The photographs accompanied Davis's frequent written reports as the project went along. The photographer was probably Nickolas Winther, whose place of business was on Commerce Street in San Antonio. He took at least 64 images between July 29, 1876, and February 4, 1878. Most of the photographs in this chapter were taken by Winther. By September 1877, some of the storerooms and the blacksmith and wheelwright shops were already in use. There was no indication of a formal end of the construction or opening ceremony. The process of construction blended into operation without stopping to celebrate.

Construction of the San Antonio Quartermaster Depot began on June 21, 1876, on 93 acres of land donated to the War Department by the City of San Antonio. This photograph shows the progress by August 12. The outline of the exterior walls has been laid out, and construction of the tower has begun. (FSHM.)

In this November 1, 1876, view, the center and eastern parts of the south side are under construction. The arches form the support for the north wall of the offices upstairs. Roofing on the western section is almost complete. To the right of the sally port, a workman can be seen on the ramp leading up to the second story. (FSHM.)

Work on the tower had progressed to almost 20 feet by August 12, 1876. As the tower went up, a four-foot-square brick shaft was constructed in the center to support the stairway, which wound around it. Within the shaft were the pipes leading to the water tank. Later, the shaft held the weights and pendulum of the clock. (FSHM.)

The south side is under construction in October 1876. The arches to support the north wall of the offices are in place while the ground-floor exterior wall is being built. The office windows have been emplaced, and the storeroom roof is sheathed. The stairwell entrance is visible, but the sally port is unfinished. (FSHM.)

By December 4, 1876, the south side of the depot was about half complete. The sally port was complete, and the plasterers were working in the second-story offices. The roof over the four western storerooms was almost complete, while the eastern part of the roof had not been framed. The tower reached the 64-foot level where the watchman's platform was located. (FSHM.)

This view through the sally port was taken just inside the heavy iron gate. At the left side is the entrance to the stairs leading up to offices on the second story. During filming for the movie *Wings*, a scene was shot at this doorway. Commemorative plaques have been mounted on the right side of the sally port. (FSHM.)

Construction of the central section, which contained the offices for the San Antonio Quartermaster Depot, is under way in September 1876. The two storerooms on either side of the sally port have three ventilation windows instead of two. The ends and back sides of the offices as well as the roof are yet to be completed. (FSHM.)

This view from the northwest corner of the depot on March 14, 1877, shows the partially completed south side of the depot and the inside corner of the western side storerooms. The roof along the southern side is complete. During the construction of the depot, some 8,500 perches, or about 7,792 cubic yards of stone, were used. (FSHM.)

Beyond the stacks of lumber, the tower has reached the 64-foot level by January 4, 1877. Atop the tower, a crane is used to lift the limestone blocks. The windows and balconies for the watchman's station are being emplaced. Beyond the tower, the roof on the southern side nears completion. (FSHM.)

Workmen carry the limestone blocks up the ramps to the top of the 24-foot-high north wall in March 1877. At the far right are the north end of the eastern storerooms and the northeast gate. This gate leads to Austin Road, now New Braunfels Avenue. (FSHM.)

Above, the east wing of the depot nears completion on March 14, 1877. The walls are complete, the roof has been framed, and the standing seam metal roofing has been applied to about half the roof. Fourteen storerooms were in each wing; 13 of them measured 30 by 40 feet. The southernmost room measured 30 by 50 feet. Below, the roof over the western storerooms, seen from the southwest on April 1, 1877, is about half complete, with the standing seam metal applied to the southern third. Note the small windows, two per room, for ventilation rather than illumination. As the headquarters grew and the storerooms were converted to offices, the windows were enlarged to match the existing upstairs office windows. (Both, FSHM.)

The roof is being installed over the storerooms in March 1877. These are the ventilation windows along the outside wall of the building, two per room and secured by bars. The wall dividing the adjacent storerooms was midway between the two windows in the center of the image. (FSHM.)

Each storeroom in the depot opened into the courtyard. The doorway was large enough for a supply wagon to be backed through it for loading or unloading. The two windows were equipped with wooden shutters. On the outer wall of the supply room were two small windows for ventilation. (FSHM.)

This April 1877 view of the depot shows the south and west sides of the building and a partially completed tower. It was taken from a point about one mile to the southwest, or near the intersection of present-day Milam and Cherry Streets. Note the absence of any civilian structures between here and the depot. (FSHM.)

By April 1877, the tower's masonry work and roof were complete. Yet to be installed was the 6,400-gallon water tank, which was filled by the pump house located at the west end of the post. A signal on the west side of the tower indicated the water level. The tank served the depot and the San Antonio National Cemetery, about 3,000 yards south of the post. (FSHM.)

The completed tower measured 90 feet from base to the eaves of the roof. It took 103 steps to reach the level of the balconies, 64 feet above the ground. The quartermaster general, Montgomery Meigs, insisted a stone tower, rather than a steel trestle, for the water tank was more appropriate for an important military installation. (FSHM.)

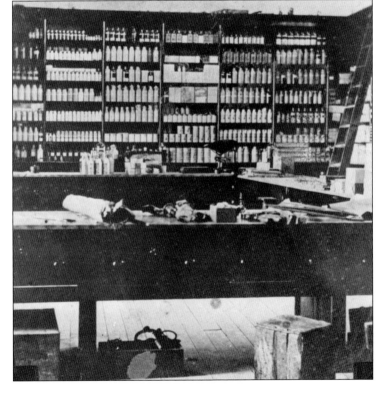

The storerooms on the south side measured 30 by 40 feet. The walls of this one, photographed on September 27, 1877, are lined with shelves well-stocked with bottles and other containers. The image is not captioned by the photographer, but this appears to be the medical storeroom. (FSHM.)

Though the depot was not completed until February 1878, some of the storage rooms, like this one shown in September 1877, were already being used. This storeroom is in the southern side of the depot. The columns are topped by arches supporting the northern wall of the staff offices upstairs. (FSHM.)

The sheds along the northwest portion of the depot are complete in this March 26, 1877, view. The sheds were used as parking areas for the wagons. To the right, the blacksmith and wheelwright shops would be constructed. At far left is one of the two northern gates. (FSHM.)

The building for the blacksmith and wheelwright shops was completed in February 1878, but the shops were already in operation by September 1877. The blacksmith shops occupied the western half of the building. Note the chimneys for the four forges. The wheelwright shops were located in the eastern half. (FSHM.)

In this February 4, 1878, view, the east wing of the Quadrangle has been completed. This image clearly shows the random-laid limestone block construction. The limestone was brought on wagons from the city rock quarries, which are currently home to the San Antonio Zoo and Sunken Garden Theater. (FSHM.)

The wheelwright shop in the Quadrangle manufactured wheels and wagon parts and repaired the wagons used by the depot and the garrison. Here, three craftsmen are working on a field ambulance in September 1878. Ambulances were occasionally used as shuttle buses to transport dependents to school on the post. (FSHM.)

A blacksmith stands by one of the forges in the blacksmith shop at the north side of the courtyard. Arrayed along the front of the forge are some of the tools used in cutting, shaping, and perforating iron stock. In addition to making and fitting horseshoes, blacksmiths could make or repair the iron components of wagons, such as wheel rims, brackets, and hooks. (FSHM.)

The central third of the south side of the depot, seen here on February 4, 1878, had four large rooms on the ground floor, two on each side of the sally port. These were used as storerooms and the printing office. Upstairs, there were nine offices used by the depot staff and the stairwell landing. (FSHM.)

This view from the watchman's station at the 64-foot level of the tower toward the offices on the south side clearly shows the standing seam metal roof and the 10-foot-wide arcade. An ornate wrought iron railing, not clearly visible here, runs along the outer edge of the arcade between the columns. (FSHM.)

Maj. Gen. Edward O.C. Ord commanded the Department of Texas during the acquisition of the land on Government Hill and the construction of the Quadrangle. He served as a division, corps, and Army commander during the Civil War. General Ord is seen here with his family at the Jefferson Davis mansion at the end of the war. (LOC.)

In the printing office, W.C. Freeman, wearing an apron, stands at the table with two other civilian employees. The printing office, on the ground floor in the fourth room east of the sally port, printed reports and produced the forms necessary to conduct the business of the headquarters and the depot. (FSHM.)

This view from the clock tower shows the shops along the north wall. Beyond are the stables for the horses and mules. These stables could accommodate 128 animals. At left are the corrals, paddocks, and hay yard. This area was surrounded by an open shed and brick wall. (FSHM.)

A convoy of wagons assembles in the stable area north of the Quadrangle. At right are the quarters for the civilian teamsters. The stables are in the background. The development of the railroad network throughout Texas, which delivered the goods faster, would put an end to this ritual. (FSHM.)

Two

THE CENTRAL POINT

After the San Antonio Quartermaster Depot moved to Government Hill, work began to modify the Quadrangle for the Department of Texas headquarters, which was still in town. The garrison of the Post at San Antonio was also in town and paying rent for barracks and officer quarters. Work began in July 1878 to extend the second story of the building the full length of the south side. This was completed in November of that year. The garrison moved to Government Hill on December 22, 1879, occupying tents and temporary buildings west of the depot. The headquarters stayed put because there were no officer quarters on Government Hill.

The War Department rectified that situation by constructing 15 sets of officer quarters west of the depot. These quarters were designed by Alfred Giles, with the largest and grandest set for the commanding general. The field grade and company grade officer quarters, smaller and less grand, were completed in the summer of 1881, whereupon the headquarters relocated to Government Hill. The staff of the depot relocated their offices to the first-floor storerooms as the headquarters moved in.

More change was in store as the War Department concentrated troops at the post. Its location made it suitable for positioning a strategic reserve of troops that could move, if needed, along the Mexican border, to an Indian uprising, or to labor troubles. Construction east of the depot between 1885 and 1894 made the Post at San Antonio (renamed Fort Sam Houston in 1890) the second-largest post in the country.

The war with Spain saw the depot mobilizing troops for overseas service and brought about the construction of the Cavalry and Light Artillery Post north of the depot. By 1912, Fort Sam Houston was the largest post in the country. Revolution in Mexico brought most of the Army to the border, to be commanded by the headquarters and supported by the depot in the Quadrangle. As these events unfolded, the headquarters and the depot expanded beyond the capability of the Quadrangle to hold them both.

Work is under way in 1878 to extend the second story of the building to the west of the sally port. The roof and framing have been stripped away, and new walls are being added. Wooden frames have been placed on the columns to support the construction of the arches. The arcade was continued along the north side of the extension. (FSHM.)

The extension of the second story over the western end of the south side of the depot continues as the walls are completed and the framing of the new roof is finished. The arcade, which was continued along the front of the new offices, featured four sets of three arches. (FSHM.)

In this view from the tower, the western extension is almost complete. The roof has been covered with standing seam metal. Work continues on the arcade and the offices. In the distance, the city of San Antonio is barely visible. This section would be occupied by the paymaster, surgeon, quartermaster, and telegraph offices. (FSHM.)

Seen from the southwest, the western wing has had its roof removed, a new floor installed over the first-floor rooms, and most of its exterior walls completed. The framing of the roof is less than one-half complete. When this section was completed, the process was repeated for the eastern wing. (FSHM.)

These two views show the south side of the Quadrangle as it was completed in February 1878 (above) and after it was modified to accommodate the staff of the Department of Texas headquarters (below). The addition doubled the space in the Quadrangle used as offices. Despite the completion of the addition to the second story, the headquarters remained in San Antonio. In 1879, Maj. Gen. Edward O.C. Ord rated the offices as sufficient, but "there are no officer quarters." After quarters were built in 1881, the headquarters moved in. The depot staff was moved to the first floor, leaving the second story for the Department of Texas staff. (Both, FSHM.)

This ground-level view shows the eastern half of the southern side of the Quadrangle from the southeast corner (left) to the sally port (right). Along the arcade in this part of the second-story addition were the offices of the commissary of subsistence, the engineer, the medical director, the judge advocate, and the inspector general. (FSHM.)

This view looking in the opposite direction shows the western portion of the south side of the Quadrangle. A man in uniform, a watchman perhaps, sits in the doorway of the stairwell leading upstairs. Next to him, a young girl stands on a chair. At either end of the building is an area marked as a "sink," or latrine. (Martin Callahan.)

This is the view looking west from the east end of the original arcade. In the 1990s, historic photographs were put up along the arcade. A copy of this image was displayed at the location from which the photograph was taken so a visitor could compare this view with the contemporary one. (FSHM.)

This view from the tower shows the parade ground, including the flagpole and St. Paul's Episcopal Church at far left. Also at far left is part of the fence that encloses the garrison officer quarters. While the staff lived in the permanent quarters, officers in the garrison lived in temporary buildings. (Martin Callahan.)

Brig. Gen. Christopher C. Augur, a veteran of the Mexican War, the Indian Wars, and the Civil War, was the commander of the Department of Texas from 1881 to 1883. He was the first occupant of the commanding general's quarters and the first officer to command the Department of Texas from the Quadrangle. (FSHM.)

Viewed from the tower are the 15 sets of quarters built west of the depot for the Department of Texas commander and staff in 1881. Upon completion of the quarters, the headquarters occupied the offices on the second floor of the Quadrangle. The largest quarters, at the bend in the road, were for the commanding general. (FSHM.)

In 1882, a clock was installed in the tower, replacing the water tank. Initially, only the south and west sides of the tower had a clockface. The addition of faces on the other sides coincided with the establishment of the Infantry Post (1885–1894) and the Cavalry and Light Artillery Post (1904–1912). (FSHM.)

The rectangular tablet below the clock face proclaims, "San Antonio Quartermaster's Depot Erected under Act of Congress A.D. 1878. In Peace Prepare for War." It then lists the names of the president, secretary of war, and Generals Sherman, Sheridan, Meigs, and Ord. The second *e* in *quartermaster* is missing on the tablet. (FSHM.)

Lt. Gen. John M. Schofield was awarded the Medal of Honor for gallantry while leading an infantry regiment in 1861. He commanded the XXIII Corps during Sherman's March to the Sea and the Atlanta Campaign. Schofield was appointed secretary of war and served as the superintendent at the US Military Academy, commander of the Department of Texas from 1883 to 1884, and commanding general of the Army from 1888 to 1895. (LOC.)

Brig. Gen. David S. Stanley, Medal of Honor recipient for gallantry in the Civil War, sits at his desk in his office, located in the second room east of the stairwell on the second story. During his tenure as department commander, 1884–1892, Fort Sam Houston grew to be the second-largest post in the country. (FSHM.)

On September 10, 1886, Apache war chief Geronimo and his band arrived in the Quadrangle. Army tents were set up for them northwest of the tower during their six-week stay. During their stay, the Apaches consumed Army rations rather than venison, and Geronimo did not jump from the tower as some people believe. (FSHM.)

Where was this 1886 picture of Geronimo taken? In 2006, the museum curator set out into the Quadrangle with a copy of the picture to match the arrangement of the limestone blocks behind Geronimo. She found that this photograph was taken to the left, or south, of the northwest gate of the Quadrangle. (FSHM.)

Viewed from the tower around 1890, the Upper Post is almost complete, lacking only two barracks, the band barracks, and the bachelor officer quarters. Just beyond the east wing of the Quadrangle are, from left to right, the garrison commander's quarters, four company grade officer quarters, and the post headquarters. (FSHM.)

In this view looking from the Upper Post back toward the Quadrangle at about the same time, the south and east side of the Quadrangle can be seen. The east side of the tower has had a clockface added. This image was taken from the second-story veranda of the garrison commander's quarters. (Martin Callahan.)

This view from the back of the Quadrangle shows the entire addition to the second story on the south side to accommodate the Department of Texas headquarters. Six rooms were added on each side of the sally port. The small structure near the west (right) side of the courtyard is the instrument station for monitoring the weather. (FSHM.)

San Antonio photographer Mary Jacobsen captured this view of the Quadrangle courtyard around 1891. In the left foreground is one of the fountains added around 1882. The landscaping by this time was quite elaborate. Just visible behind the tower is the shed for the hose cart in case of fire. (Martin Callahan.)

Maj. Peter D. Vroom, inspector general of the Department of Texas, sits in a carriage near the southwest corner of the Quadrangle. The three women in the carriage are identified only as, from left to right, Dollie, Kitty, and Mazy. Vroom served as inspector general of the Army in 1903. (FSHM.)

This view of the Quadrangle was taken from the second story of the bachelor officer quarters at the entrance to the Upper Post between 1894 and 1906. The intersection of Grayson Street and New Braunfels Avenue is just outside the gate at left. Note that few of the ventilation windows have been enlarged, indicating that the staff has not yet moved into these storerooms. (FSHM.)

This c. 1890 view of the clock tower from the vicinity of the sally port shows some of the changes at the Quadrangle. The original blacksmith and wheelwright shops are gone, moved to the stables area north of the Quadrangle. A ring of bollards connected by a chain runs around the base of the tower. (FSHM.)

A mule-drawn ambulance exits the sally port in 1895. Some of the small ventilation windows on the ground floor have been enlarged to admit more light. This reflects the conversion of storerooms into offices. In this case, it was for the quartermaster staff that was displaced by the Department of Texas staff in 1881. (FSHM.)

For most of the period after the garrison of the Post at San Antonio arrived on Government Hill, there was an artillery battery on post without a proper place to store its equipment. In 1892, this gun shed was built outside the northeast corner of the Quadrangle with bays for the guns, limbers, and ammunition caissons of the battery. (FSHM.)

Between 1891 and 1893, new stables and shops were built in the area north of the quadrangle and with a brick wall enclosing this area. The original blacksmith and wheelwright shops were demolished. Note the scattering of civilian structures to the north and east of the Quadrangle. San Antonio is beginning to surround Fort Sam Houston. (FSHM.)

Pvt. Charles Ryan, Light Battery F, 3rd Artillery, stands by a Model 1885 3.2-inch field gun outside the north wall of the Quadrangle on December 9, 1895. The Model 1895 gun used an interrupted screw breech and could fire a shell 5,970 meters. This gun was the first rifled steel breechloader in US service. (FSHM.)

Pvt. ? Saunders stands with his horse, Dude, outside the gun shed next to the Quadrangle in 1895. Saunders wears the five-button sack coat and kepi typical of the late 1880s. He carries an M1840 light artillery saber and a Colt revolver on his belt. Dude is equipped with the M1885 McClellan saddle. (FSHM.)

Two soldiers from Light Battery F, 3rd Artillery square off for an impromptu boxing match outside the north wall of the Quadrangle on December 9, 1895, while their comrades look on. The battery's stables and gun shed, where the cannon, limbers, and caissons were parked, were located outside the northeast corner of the Quadrangle. (FSHM.)

Bessie Taylor, second from the left, poses in the Quadrangle in 1903 with her friends, from left to right, Polly DeRaismes, Elise Gransteller, and Elizabeth O'Keefe. Bessie's father, Col. Sidney W. Taylor, served as the adjutant general of the Department of Texas and lived on the Staff Post with his wife and four daughters. (FSHM.)

Lt. William Westervelt stands at the entrance to the Upper Post on Grayson Street around 1903 with the Quadrangle in the background. A field artillery officer, Westervelt would chair the Westervelt Board, which developed the post–World War I plan to modernize the field artillery of the US Army. (FSHM.)

In this view looking from the tower to the southeast in 1903, one can see the almost fully developed Upper Post. The post headquarters building is at the lower end of the flagpole. To the left are officer quarters; to the right, bachelor officer quarters. San Antonio has grown right up to the south side of the Quadrangle. (FSHM.)

Another view from the tower in 1903, this one—almost due east—shows the "long barracks" and sally port of the Upper Post. The large house in the left middle ground is the quarters for the commanding officer of the garrison of the Upper Post. It was home for Brig. Gen. Joseph W. "Vinegar Joe" Stilwell from 1939 to 1940. (FSHM.)

Department commander Brig. Gen. Jesse M. Lee sits with his staff in the Quadrangle in 1904. From left to right are (seated) Maj. R.R. Stevens, Col. John Putnam, Brig. Gen. Jesse M. Lee, Maj. John L. Bullis, and Maj. W.S. Finley; (standing) Lieutenants ? McCaskey and ? Moseley, Maj. H.D. Snyder, Capt. S.B. Boots, Capt. Guy Carleton, Capt. L.J. Fleming, and Capt. C.D. Roberts. (FSHM.)

Between 1898 and 1900, a rectangular pond was built in the southeast corner of the Quadrangle. Shown here on a pre-1907 postcard, the island in the pond is covered with foliage. By 1907, a small house or shelter for the water fowl had replaced the foliage on the island. (FSHM.)

Swans swim in one of the two fountains that flank the central driveway in the courtyard. The fountains were installed shortly after the Quadrangle was built. By the First World War, the fountains were removed. At far right is a structure over one of the cisterns. Just to the left is the weather instrument station. (FSHM.)

A 17668 Sally Port, Fort Sam Houston, San Antonio, Tex

Albert H. Patrick
9 Inf. Band

In this ground level view of the southwest corner of the Quadrangle, few of the west wing windows have been enlarged, indicating that the headquarters staff has not expanded into this area yet. The 1904 water tank can be seen to the right of the tower, which still has the original clock. (FSHM.)

11876 Drive Way Lower Post, Water Towers in Distance, Fort Sam Houston, Texas.

Rec'd your letter some time ago. Glad you are all so well.
It has been delightful here all winter, can sit out nearly
every day without a wrap. Love to you all. Your cousin James

This is the view looking east from the Lower, or Staff, Post, toward the Quadrangle from a postcard postmarked 1906. The 1900 and 1904 water tanks can be seen but the clock tower is concealed by the foliage at the right. The driveway to the left goes to the post hospital. (FSHM.)

This pre-1907 view of the Quadrangle interior show more changes along the north wall. A signal service shop was added in 1893 to the west side of the tower and storage sheds to the east side. The signal service building, identified by its four sets of double doors, also included the weather observation station. (FSHM.)

In this view from the tower, the Cavalry and Light Artillery Post addition, built between 1905 and 1912, is visible beyond the stables, constructed in the 1890s. Fort Sam Houston became a brigade post and the largest post in the country. Along the inside of the north wall are the signal service shop (left) and a storage shed. (FSHM.)

At left in this photograph is a shed over one of the two underground cisterns. In 1912, the three steel tanks and the cisterns held 831,000 gallons of water. The growth of the installation can be seen as the amount of water in the depot grew from 6,400 gallons in 1878 to 831,000 gallons by 1912. (FSHM.)

While the fountains and pond added to the scenic nature of the Quadrangle, the water tanks were ugly and purely functional. They supplied water for the horses and mules of the depot and the garrison, which by 1912 included a regiment each of cavalry and infantry and a battalion of artillery. Water was also necessary for firefighting. (FSHM.)

This 1913 postmarked card shows the clock tower and the water tanks added in 1904 (right) and 1911. Already enlarged into a brigade post, Fort Sam Houston was planned as a concentration site for a 12,000-man division of troops in the event of a mobilization like the one in 1911. (FSHM.)

A soldier stands with a group of civilians in the southwest corner of the Quadrangle. The Commissary Department still operated from this area of the depot. Most of the people working in the depot were civilian employees, including women. This is evident by a building identified on post maps as the ladies' latrine. (FSHM.)

This post-1914 postcard shows the eastern wing of the Quadrangle along what is now New Braunfels Avenue. All the small ventilation windows have been enlarged, indicating that the entire wing is in use as office space. The small building at left is the officer's mess, previously a set of officer quarters moved here from the Staff Post around 1885. (FSHM.)

Brig. Gen. Frederick Funston, a Medal of Honor recipient, commanded the Southern Department from 1915 to 1917. Operations along the Mexican border and the Punitive Expedition highlighted his tenure in the Quadrangle. He is also responsible for extending the second story of the Quadrangle even farther to the east to provide him more office space. (LOC.)

Maj. Gen. John J. Pershing, Southern Department commander, rides in a Buick touring car in the 1917 Battle of Flowers Parade with, from left to right, architect Atlee Ayers, president of the Fiesta San Jacinto Association; Brig Gen. Henry Hutchins, state adjutant general of Texas; and Gov. James E. Ferguson, of Texas. (FSHM.)

Quadrangle, Fort Sam Houston, San Antonio, Texas.

This postcard view of the Quadrangle courtyard appears in a World War I portfolio that includes scenes of training at Camp Travis, the Gift Chapel at Fort Sam Houston, and aircraft at Kelly Field. Deer, a peacock, and other fowl are gathered near the structure over the cistern in the southwest corner. (FSHM.)

Three

A HUB OF MILITARY ACTIVITY

After the First World War, the Southern Department was reorganized as the VIII Corps Area. In 1917, the Army had realized that the requirements of supporting military operations in the Southwest and along the Mexican border could not be accomplished in the Quadrangle any longer as those requirements had increased geometrically while the headquarters was expanding to manage the expanded activity. The neighborhood east of the Quadrangle, totaling some 103 acres, was purchased and demolished to make way for new warehouses and facilities for the depot. Only one civilian building was spared. Kraus's Meat Market on New Braunfels Avenue survived to become the Quartermaster Sales Meat Branch. By the end of the war, only the Signal Corps warehouse had been completed. The new depot area was finished and occupied in 1922, leaving only the headquarters in the Quadrangle.

As the sole occupant of the Quadrangle, the VIII Corps Area headquarters brought the courtyard back to its parklike appearance. The deer and fowl again attracted visitors, both locals and tourists. The Quadrangle also attracted Hollywood, as scenes for the movie *Wings* were filmed in the courtyard in 1926. *Wings* was the first film to receive the Academy Award for Best Picture. Hollywood returned in 1941 for the filming of *Soldiers in White*. But there was serious business going on as well. The headquarters had to manage the reduction of the postwar Army in terms of manpower and installations as budgets shrank. As the Great Depression swept over the country, the Army was tasked with supporting the Civilian Conservation Corps (CCC) logistically and with cadres of Army officers and noncommissioned officers for the CCC companies in a five-state area, with 42 companies in Texas alone.

As war approached, the headquarters conducted large-scale maneuvers in Louisiana. Mobilization had begun. During the war, Fourth Army moved into the Quadrangle and generated the headquarters of the Ninth, Tenth, and Fifteenth Armies. Out of Quadrangle came Gens. Walter Krueger, Courtney Hodges, William Simpson, and Dwight Eisenhower, all of whom commanded armies or larger organizations overseas.

More than a dozen deer and a peacock can be seen grazing in the northern part of the Quadrangle in this 1920 photograph. A muzzle-loading cannon, which was emplaced sometime between 1890 and 1900, can be seen to the left of the tower with its caisson on the other side. (FSHM.)

This deer seems unconcerned about being petted by a woman visiting the Quadrangle. Note the part of the building just beyond the woman's right shoulder. As the second story extends to the end of the first story, this dates the photograph after 1916 when General Funston added another room to the second floor in the southeast corner. (FSHM.)

The visitor is seen here again, this time at the pond with one of the swans. At this point in time, the foliage on the island has been replaced by a little house. Note the small bridge from the side of the pond to the island. Problems with the pond leaking would cause its replacement during Lieutenant General Wiggins's tenure, from 2013 to 2016. (FSHM.)

This lady continues her visit to the Quadrangle, strolling among the deer and fowl. The building to her left is the telegraph office. Originally, the telegraph line went into the Signal Officer's room on the second story. The telegraph office was repurposed a few times before its eventual demolition in 1960. (FSHM.)

This panoramic view and the one that follows show the appearance of the Quadrangle in 1916 and in 1919. Here, the hustle and bustle of the supply activities of the depot are evident. With

both the headquarters and the depot activity expanding, one or the other would have to move to a larger facility. (FSHM.)

On February 18, 1919, the officers, enlisted men, and civilian employees of the Southern Department headquarters turned out for a group photograph in the Quadrangle. The number of people on

the staff had proliferated since 1881, and they took over most of the building. The entire staff in 1881 would have barely filled up the chairs in the front row. (FSHM.)

James E. Fechet enlisted in the cavalry and was wounded at San Juan Hill in 1898. He transferred to the Signal Corps and served with the Air Service during World War I. Fechet served in the Quadrangle as the Southern Department aviation officer from 1919 to 1920 and, as a major general, was chief of the Air Service from 1927 to 1931. (LOC.)

One of the resident peacocks strolls across the driveway in the southeast corner of the Quadrangle. Peacocks (more correctly peafowl) begin to appear in photographs around 1916. Though there is no explanation for their introduction into the Quadrangle, the tail feathers of these birds are highly prized by visitors. (FSHM.)

Maj. Gen. Joseph T. Dickman was commander of the Southern Department when it became the VIII Corps Area. Previously, he had served in the Geronimo campaign, the Spanish-American War, and the Philippine Insurrection. During the First World War, he commanded, in turn, the 3rd Division, the IV Corps, and the Third Army in France. (LOC.)

A cowboy troubadour sings and plays a guitar in the Quadrangle. His presence is indicative of the way the people of San Antonio viewed the Quadrangle and Fort Sam Houston. Fort Sam Houston was San Antonio's Army post, and the people felt at home going there. Some even picnicked on the grounds on weekends. (FSHM.)

In this 1920 view of the southwestern part of the Quadrangle, all the former ventilation windows on the ground floor have been converted to full-size ones. The window frames at the end of the west wing and the two to the right were cut into the walls where no windows had existed before. (FSHM.)

This ground-level view of the southeast corner of the Quadrangle from across New Braunfels Avenue shows the second-story addition for General Funston. The addition would eventually be converted into a conference room for the commanding general, whose office was adjacent to it. The fence conceals a fountain added around 1906. (FSHM.)

This temporary building was erected in 1916 in the northwest corner. It provided additional office space for the depot staff during operations along the border and the mobilization after Pancho Villa's raid. It would continue in use after 1922 in a variety of non-depot activities until it was demolished in 1960. (FSHM.)

The telegraph office, located in the southwest corner of the courtyard of the Quadrangle, was erected in 1916. At the time, Major General Funston's headquarters were communicating with units all along the Mexican border, with Brigadier General Pershing's forces operating in Mexico, and with the installations within the Southern Department. (FSHM.)

In this 1920 view of the west wing of the Quadrangle, the storeroom doors have been replaced by doors with sidelights and fanlights. At far left, one of the original windows has been converted into a doorway. There is not a horse in sight as motorcars have become common. (FSHM.)

VISITORS
ARE PROHIBITED FROM
ANNOYING WATER-FOWL OR DEER
UNDER PENALTY OF
BEING EXPELLED FROM GROUNDS

With the Quadrangle looking more like a park than a major military headquarters involved in serious matters like national defense, a swan swims toward the warning sign next to the pond. The stern tone of the warning would indicate that some visitors had previously acted improperly toward the Quadrangle animals. (FSHM.)

Maj. Gen. John L. Hines followed General Dickman as VIII Corps Area commander from 1921 to 1922. He had served in the war with Spain and the Philippine Insurrection. He was General Pershing's adjutant during the Punitive Expedition. During the First World War, Hines commanded a brigade in the 1st Division, the 4th Division, and the III Corps Area. He later became Army chief of staff in 1924. (LOC.)

Former Indian scout Joe Harris directs traffic at the Quadrangle sally port in this pre–World War I photograph. During his military service and civilian employment in San Antonio, he worked for 31 general officers. The first was Maj. Gen. Joseph J. Reynolds, commander of the Department of Texas in 1871. The last was Brig. Gen. Albert J. Bowley, commander of the 2nd Division in 1928. (FSHM.)

This view of the sally port in the 1920s shows gateman Joe Harris seated in his chair. The sign at the left side of the sally port advises motorcyclists that they must use the gates at the northeast and northwest corners of the Quadrangle and park near the water towers. (FSHM.)

On a sunny Sunday afternoon, October 16 1921, visitors stroll about the Quadrangle with not a single soldier in sight. Visitors would often go up in the tower to the stand on the balcony. Today, visitors must sign a release form approved by the staff judge advocate before ascending the 103 steps. (FSHM.)

The west side of the Quadrangle, viewed from the Staff Post parade ground, has had all the former storerooms converted to offices. All the small ventilation windows have been enlarged. Headquarters growth was not due to bureaucratic bloat but to the addition of staff to handle new missions and responsibilities. (LOC.)

Col. William A. Mitchell, outspoken advocate for air power, served as aviation officer in the VIII Corps Area from 1925 until he resigned from the Army following his court-martial for insubordination. His office in the Quadrangle now serves as an artifact storage room of the Fort Sam Houston Museum. (FSHM.)

Mounted in front of the tower is a bronze plaque with the Gettysburg Address. It would soon be mounted at the base of the tower and eventually inside the sally port. An old-timer visiting the Fort Sam Houston Museum in the 1980s said that the two water tanks were named Niles and Stevens after "the two biggest drunks in the Army." (FSHM.)

Though San Antonio is known for its fine weather, Mother Nature occasionally gives the Alamo City a light dusting of snow, like this one around 1925. The two soldiers at the gate are all bundled up with not much traffic to direct. The city would get its record snowfall in 1985. (FSHM.)

Running along the west side of the Quadrangle, this road leads to the Cavalry and Light Artillery Post. In 1934, this street would be named Liscum Road in honor of Col. Emerson Liscum, 9th Infantry, who was killed in action at the Battle of Tientsin during the China Relief Expedition in 1900. (LOC.)

Plans had been in place since 1916 to enclose the arcade along the eastern and western ends of the south side of the Quadrangle. When this was finally accomplished, the area within the arches was filled with fanlights of the same pattern used on the doorways from the offices into the courtyard. Note the telephone booth to the right of the sally port. (LOC.)

In 1927, the United Services Automobile Association (USAA) bought the property across Grayson Street from the southwest corner of the Quadrangle. Here, in 1928, it would start to build its second corporate headquarters. After several expansions to the building, USAA relocated and sold it to the Army in 1959. It became Building 44, Fourth Army Annex. (FSHM.)

The VIII Corps Area commander, Maj. Gen. Ernest Hinds, second from right, stands next to Generaloberst Wilhelm Heye, Chef der Heeresleitung (head of the army command) of the German Reichswehr, near the Wars Plans Division office on the arcade in the Quadrangle in 1927. The other two gentlemen are their aides-de-camp. (FSHM.)

In 1927, a sundial was emplaced on the sidewalk in front of the tower. It was made by Ernesto Vidales, former Signal Corps sergeant and civil service employee in the Quadrangle. Transferred to Kelly Field, Vidales was the first Hispanic American to serve as a foreman there. He retired in 1957. (FSHM.)

The War Department authorized purchase of land for a new depot in 1917. The new depot area included 38 warehouses aggregating 608,000 square feet, an office building on New Braunfels Avenue, and a gasoline station. Capacity of the new depot area was sufficient to replace all the rented storage space in the city. (FSHM.)

This aerial view looking north at the Quadrangle and vicinity was taken in early 1931. Clockwise from the top are the former stables (now motor sheds) of the Cavalry and Light Artillery Post, the new depot area, the Infantry Post, San Antonio along Grayson Street, and the Staff Post. (FSHM.)

Note the increasing number of automobiles parked in the Quadrangle. The presence of the Vidales sundial and Gettysburg Address plaque date this photograph after 1927. The license plate on the car at lower right is illegible but is in the format of the 1931 Texas license plates. (FSHM.)

Parked in the back of the Quadrangle is this Packard luxury, four-door touring car with a convertible top. The car bears the white numerals 66-405 on the green background of the 1932 Texas license plate, with a Press tag below it. Attached to the radiator is a medallion for the Benevolent and Protective Order of Elks. (FSHM.)

The VIII Corps Area signal section has parked its parade float in the Quadrangle. It depicts the old radio room and pigeon loft as well as the two radio towers on the Cavalry and Light Artillery Post. The Army had been an active participant in the San Antonio Fiesta parades since 1891. (FSHM.)

These two views of the VIII Corps Area signal office show the state-of-the-art Army communications in the 1930s. Located in the northernmost rooms in the west wing, this office served both telephone and radio systems. Above, a telephone switchboard sits in the center of the room. Radio receivers are located on the far wall. Below, three soldiers man the radio sets. The antenna field for the radios was located at the north end of the post. The system of wires and pulleys overhead carried written messages throughout the office. One device found on every desk but not found in the communications center in the Quadrangle today is the ashtray. (Both, FSHM.)

Changes had taken place in the buildings added inside the Quadrangle in 1916. In this 1935 aerial view by Carl Ekmark, the telegraph office in the southwest corner had been converted to the CCC construction office and the office in the northwest corner was occupied by the finance department. (FSHM.)

This 1930s view of the Quadrangle courtyard from the arcade is unusual in that no deer or fowl are visible. The cannon, a 12- or 18-pound gun emplaced in the 1890s, can be seen to the right front of the tower. Its caisson, emplaced to the left of the tower, is concealed by the foliage. (FSHM.)

In 1944, Lt. Gen. William H. Simpson brought the Fourth Army headquarters to the Quadrangle, replacing the Third Army. During his tenure, the Fourth Army provided the cadre for the Ninth Army, which he would command in the European theater. The Fourth Army later furnished cadres for the Tenth and Fifteenth Armies. (FSHM.)

Wartime security during the Second World War seems to have curtailed photography in the Quadrangle. No photographs by Carl Ekmark and no personal photographs have yet found their way into the Fort Sam Houston Museum's collections. This October 1944 image of the Quadrangle wildlife was taken by the Signal Corps. (FSHM.)

Four

NATIONAL HISTORIC LANDMARK

The Quadrangle began the postwar period with the Fourth Army in command of all Army forces and installations in a five-state area. These installations included a large part of the Army's artillery at Fort Sill, Oklahoma; air defense artillery at Fort Bliss, Texas; and aviation at Fort Wolters, Texas, as well as the armored force at Fort Hood, Texas. This aggregation of forces and the numerical designation of the headquarters in the Quadrangle gave birth to one of the Fourth Army's nicknames: the "Quad-A Army"—for its artillery, air defense, aviation, and armor. It was also called the "Missile Army" for its control of Forts Sill and Bliss. During this time, the deputy commanding general of the Fourth Army served as the post commander of Fort Sam Houston. Fort Sam Houston had started to change as the Army began transferring medical training activities there, beginning with the Medical Field Service School in 1947.

During the Cold War and the Korean War, Fourth Army mobilized Reserve Component units and increased the output of its training centers to furnish trained units and individuals as the United States reinforced the North Atlantic Treaty Organization and fought to halt Communist aggression in Korea. It deployed troops from Forts Hood, Bliss, and Sill to Florida in anticipation of an invasion of Cuba during the 1961 Cuban Missile Crisis. There was more of the same during the Vietnam War. In a postwar reorganization, the Fourth and Fifth Army areas were merged and the Fourth Army's colors were furled. Fifth Army moved its headquarters into the Quadrangle, managing the training of the Reserve Component units in the central third of the country.

In 1974, the Department of the Interior announced that Fort Sam Houston was a National Historic Landmark for its long and distinguished contributions to the history of the United States. A historic marker was emplaced across from the flagpole on Arthur MacArthur Field. Starting in 1991, steps were undertaken to emphasize the Quadrangle's status as a National Historic Landmark. The most controversial measure was the elimination of parking in the courtyard.

The Fourth Army Band begins a left turn as it leads the pass in review held in honor of Lt. Gen. John P. Lucas. As a lieutenant, General Lucas and his platoon were instrumental in repelling Pancho Villa's raid on Columbus, New Mexico, in 1916. He commanded the VI Corps in Italy during World War II. (FSHM.)

Troops pass in review for Lt. Gen. John P. Lucas on June 17, 1946, in the Quadrangle. General Lucas, commanding general of the Fourth Army, and other members of the reviewing party can be seen at far left. The troops in the foreground are carrying M-1 carbines at sling arms. (FSHM.)

Seated front and center and flanked by two Army nurses, Gen. Jonathan M. Wainwright poses in the Quadrangle in 1946 with the Wainwright Travelers. This was a group of soldiers who had served in the Philippines with him during the Second World War and who accompanied him to Fort Sam Houston. (FSHM.)

Gen. Jonathan M. Wainwright, commanding general of the Fourth Army and Medal of Honor recipient for gallantry during the defense of Bataan and Corregidor in the Philippines, stands in his office holding his saber, which was surrendered to the Japanese in 1942 at the fall of Corregidor. The saber was recently returned to him. (FSHM.)

General Wainwright and the officers and enlisted men of the Fourth Army headquarters pose for a group photograph on February 26, 1947. Wainwright, nicknamed "Skinny" even before his weight loss as a POW, sits in the center with his cane propped against his leg. Most of the officers seated in the front row wear the service uniform referred to as "pinks and greens." The enlisted

men wear the "Ike jacket." General Wainwright retired from the Army in 1947 and lived in San Antonio. His health compromised by almost four years as a prisoner of the Japanese, he died of a stroke in 1953. (FSHM.)

In the early 1950s, the Fourth Army printed Christmas cards using this photograph of one of the snow-covered M1902 guns outside the sally port. A green wreath of holly, finished off with the red-and-white Fourth Army insignia and a wide bow of red ribbon, complete the picture. (FSHM.)

M.Sgt. James Gorsuch shows his 10-year-old son Edwin the Gettysburg Address plaque in the Quadrangle sally port in 1954. These plaques were manufactured starting in 1909 at Rock Island Arsenal for the national cemeteries to commemorate the 50th anniversary of President Lincoln's address after the Battle of Gettysburg. (FSHM.)

The Fourth Army color guard stands in front of the sally port around 1955. Behind them are, from left to right, the state flags of the five states in the Fourth Army area—Arkansas, Oklahoma, Texas, Louisiana, and New Mexico. Rearranged, the initials of the states spell *Talon*, giving rise to another Fourth Army nickname, "Talon of the American Eagle." (FSHM.)

The Fourth Degree General Assembly and three councils of San Antonio Knights of Columbus were guests of honor on April 3, 1955, at a formal guard mount in the Quadrangle after the Knights made a presentation to the chaplains at Fort Sam Houston. This was followed by a band concert. (FSHM.)

Francis Beck feeds some of the Quadrangle deer in 1956. This cannon is an M1841 six-pounder gun, but the carriage was modified by the addition of M1902 wheels after the original wheels deteriorated from exposure to the weather. Polishing the cannon tube had also erased most of the manufacturer's marks. (FSHM.)

During the Fiesta de San Antonio in April 1957, the Fiesta Rockettes dance for the crowd. As the ceremonies and the crowds grew over the years, the Quadrangle was unable to host this annual event. The festivities moved to Arthur MacArthur Field. Note the small house on the island in the pond. (FSHM.)

Some of the incremental changes to the Quadrangle can be seen in these two very similar photographs taken in 1954, above, and 1958, below. Traffic signals have been added at the top of the arch in the sally port and to the right side. The lettering on the shield above the sally port has been changed from "Fourth Army" to "Fourth US Army," reflecting an organization and mission change. The shield was first put above the arch by the VIII Corps Area and can be seen in the Warner Bros. 1942 short film *Soldiers in White,* as 2nd Division soldiers march through the sally port. (Both, FSHM.)

Because it commanded the Field Artillery and Missile Center and School and the Air Defense Artillery Center and School, Fourth Army was called the "Missile Army." To highlight this mission, the missile monument was erected west of the Quadrangle in 1960. From left to right are the Corporal, Nike-Ajax, and Nike Hercules missiles. An Honest John, a Little John, and a Redstone were added later. (FSHM.)

By 1960, the clearing out of temporary buildings in and around the Quadrangle had begun. The office in the northwest corner was gone, and the telegraph office was soon to be demolished. To the north, demolition of the stables-turned-motor sheds and the World War II mobilization buildings would take another two decades. (FSHM.)

Maj. Gen. Ralph M. Osborne troops the line during a ceremony in the Quadrangle on June 12, 1961. At his right is Capt. Charles P. Flanagan with Maj. Gen. Donald P. Booth following. The captain and the color party wear the abbreviated khaki uniform, featuring shorts and knee socks. (FSHM.)

In the early 1960s, this tank—officially a Tank, Medium, Full-tracked, 90-mm Gun, M48, manufactured in 1953—was added to the missile monument. When Fort Sam Houston became a National Historic Monument, there was concern that the "modern" missiles were inappropriate in a Victorian-era neighborhood. There was less concern about the tank, which was actually more modern than the missiles. (FSHM.)

In 1948, the Fourth Army acquired two M1902 three-inch field guns from the salvage yard at Camp Stanley, Texas, and emplaced them in front of the sally port facing the Grayson Street entrance. This snow-covered gun, manufactured in 1906 at the Rock Island Arsenal, is shown here in February 1964. (FSHM.)

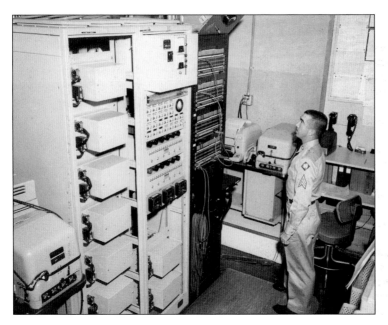

A sergeant keeps an eye on the equipment in the Fourth Army communications center in 1964. Thought it includes several teletype machines, the communications center still relies on the traditional telephone switchboard. Compare this set up with those in 1930 on page 74. Communications have certainly advanced in just three decades. (FSHM.)

This mid-1960s photograph shows not only the Quadrangle but also the surrounding area—the new depot area in the upper left, the mobilization temporaries beyond the north wall, four of the six missiles (from left to right, Nike-Ajax, Redstone, Corporal, and Nike Hercules) in the missile monument, and the former USAA building at far right. (FSHM.)

The Fife and Drum Corps of the 3rd Infantry Regiment, the "Old Guard," passes in review with measured step at the Fourth Army retreat ceremony in the Quadrangle during the 1967 Fiesta de San Antonio. This corps is part of the Army's official ceremonial unit, based at Fort Myer, Virginia. (FSHM.)

Above, in 1967, a fallow deer named Snoopy falls in with the Fourth US Army Band as it marches during a ceremony honoring Ben H. Wooten for 50 years of civilian service to the Army. Quadrangle animals often take part in ceremonies, though their participation is seldom invited. They are occasionally humorous, however. Below, Snoopy inspects the alignment and uniforms of this platoon of Fourth US Army soldiers. In later years, the animal caretaker would herd the deer into pens along the north side of the Quadrangle to reduce their interference with events. Such measures were not possible with the peafowl, which would perch in the trees and sound off. (FSHM.)

Lonnie Dempsey, an employee of the Post Engineers, makes an adjustment on the clock mechanism in the tower in 1969. This clock, installed in 1907, was the second one to be emplaced in the tower. The first clock had been installed in 1882, replacing the 6,400-gallon water tank. (FSHM.)

The deer and fowl often took shelter from the sun under the cars parked in the Quadrangle, with occasionally bad results when drivers pulled out without checking for animals under their cars. This was one of the reasons that cars were banned from parking in the Quadrangle by Lt. Gen. Neal T. Jaco. (FSHM.)

Contingents from foreign armed services often tour military installations in the United States. On October 30, 1970, this group of officers (in the light-color shirts) and enlisted men from the Coldstream Guards visited Fourth Army. Above, a specialist 5th class gives a briefing on the Quadrangle to the guardsmen. Below, a guardsman poses with one of the deer at the base of the water tower. The Coldstream Guards, formed in 1650 as Colonel Monck's Regiment of Foot, is the oldest regiment in continuous existence in the modern British army. The regimental motto is *Nulli Secundus* (Second to None). (Both, FSHM.)

More subtle changes at the sally port can be seen in this post-1971 photograph. The shield now has the Fifth Army insignia and lettering. The traffic signal has been changed, and there is a wrought iron fence along the left side of the sally port to protect pedestrians and to direct them past the noncommissioned officer in the entrance to the stairwell. (FSHM.)

In 1947, the Quadrangle had been air-conditioned. To do this, the arcade along the second story had to be enclosed. The arched sections had been closed previously with windows resembling the fan and side lights of the storeroom doors. Seen here in 1973, the center section was closed with wooden siding and aluminum frame windows, which were not sensitive to the historic architecture of the building. (FSHM.)

Surrounded by a group of peahens, one of the Quadrangle's resident peacocks displays his plumage. The peahens do not at this point look very impressed. Each year, when the peacocks shed, visitors as well as people working in the Quadrangle eagerly pick up the colorful tail feathers. (FSHM.)

In the northwest corner of the Quadrangle, Zula Hopkins discusses the Vidales sundial with Capt. Efton F. Geary, a reservist serving a tour on active duty with the Fifth Army, on September 17, 1974. Hopkins's father, Ernesto Vidales, created the sundial. The inscription on the sundial reads, "Time, devourer of all things." (FSHM.)

The command corridor on the second floor of the Quadrangle in this 1976 photograph has been decorated with a display of photographs of the commanders who have exercised command from this building. The commanding general's office is located after the third group of photographs from the right. The drop ceiling, common at that time, conceals the original beadboard ceiling. (FSHM.)

The Quadrangle Oak, selected as the second-most historic tree in Bexar County during the US bicentennial, stands in the southeast corner of the Quadrangle. The historical marker reads, in part, "Like the oak, the post has grown and developed, sinking its roots deep and spreading its influence far and wide." (FSHM.)

In 1980, the Historic American Buildings Survey paid a visit to Fort Sam Houston to document several of the historic buildings on the post, including the Quadrangle. In the sally port, at left, a fence separates pedestrian and vehicular traffic. It also directs pedestrians to the entrance of the stairwell where a noncommissioned officer controls access to the offices upstairs. The traffic signal is controlled by this noncommissioned officer. Below, this view of the southwest corner shows the doorway of the medical advisor at left and the Public Affairs Office doorway on the right. Between them is the entrance to the public restrooms. (Both, HABS.)

Above, the doorway at the western end of the arcade leads to the offices of Army Readiness Region VII. This office was involved in supporting the training of the Army Reserve and National Guard in the Fifth Army area. Some of the doorways have been blocked to limit access to a single entrance. At right, this stairwell in the southeast corner of the Quadrangle terminates in front of the room added for General Funston. The added room was used as the commanding general's conference room. Vending machines have been installed for the convenience of the staff as there is no dining facility or snack bar nearby. (Both, HABS.)

As the storerooms in the Quadrangle were converted into office space for the headquarters, the original heavy wooden double doors were replaced by human-scale doorways with fanlights and sidelights to admit more light. Originally, the woodwork was painted a light color, but that was repainted dark by 1920 and light again by the 1950s. This doorway once led to the office of Brig. Gen. Billy Mitchell. (HABS.)

This Historic American Buildings Survey photograph shows the clock tower in 1980. Flanking the entrance are the two Model 1840 cannons, acquired from Army-Navy Hospital in Little Rock, Arkansas, in 1956. The two flagpoles, emplaced on September 27, 1966, fly the United States flag and Texas state flag. The bronze plaque to the right of the door commemorates the consolidation of the Fourth and Fifth Armies in 1971. (HABS.)

In this view, the growth of the city of San Antonio since the tower was built is evident by the skyline. From left to right are the Tower of the Americas, built for Hemisfair in 1968; the Marriott Riverwalk and the Palacio del Rio Hotels; and downtown office buildings. Compare this view with the 1878 view on page 29. (FSHM.)

In this aerial view of the Quadrangle from 1982, the courtyard has been cleared of all the intrusive structures except the two water tanks. The temporary buildings, which replaced the stables, are also gone. In the lower-left corner of the photograph is the roof of the former USAA building. (FSHM.)

The drill team from the 3rd Infantry Regiment, "the Old Guard," performs a series of precision evolutions in the Quadrangle during the Fiesta de San Antonio in April 1984. In the background, the deteriorated condition of the 1911 water tank can be seen. Both of the steel tanks were removed later that year. (FSHM.)

The Fifth Army Color Guard stands before the clock tower in 1984. The Army Field Flag (at center) bears all the campaign streamers awarded to the US Army. The Fifth Army flag (right) bears the Naples-Foggia, Rome-Arno, North-Apennines, and Po Valley campaign streamers awarded to the Fifth Army for its service in Italy in World War II. (FSHM.)

This is the view of the Quadrangle from across Grayson Street in 1986. The curved limestone walls and the columns with bronze shields lettered "Fort Sam Houston" at the entrance to the driveway from Grayson Street to the sally port were added in 1940. They match the columns supporting the arches over the main entrances to the post. (FSHM.)

Lt. Gen. William Schneider, Fifth Army commander, and author-historian T.R. Fehrenbach unveil the plaque identifying the Quadrangle as part of the Fort Sam Houston National Historic Landmark in 1989. General Schneider was the first native of San Antonio to serve as the commander of the headquarters in the Quadrangle. (FSHM.)

These two 1990 views show the modifications in progress to one of the former storerooms in the Quadrangle. Above, the entrance doorway leads into a large administrative area to receive and screen visitors. Entry from the outside requires the use of an electronic key card. To the right are the entrances to a series of cubicles. Below, in a view looking in the opposite direction, are two cubicle offices and two common use areas. At far right is the vault door leading into the more secure part of the emergency operations center corridor from which Fifth Army would exercise control of its operations. (Both, FSHM.)

In what looks like a scene from Alfred Hitchcock's *The Birds*, pigeons swarm toward these three visitors. In addition to the peafowl, ducks, swans, and other fowl, the Quadrangle was often visited by migratory birds or swarmed by pigeons, as seen above and below. The pigeons come to feed on the birdseed scattered about to feed the peacocks and other resident fowl. Visitors to the Quadrangle bringing bread or other items to feed the pigeons add to the problem. Rubber snakes were emplaced on window sills to scare away the pigeons. Unfortunately, these fake predators lost their effectiveness when they were painted over during routine maintenance of the building. (Both, FSHM.)

The Fifth US Army Band turns out in its dress blue uniforms at the sally port with the drum major front and center. The drum major's baldric, or sash, is in the colors red over white. This combination has been used since World War I on heraldic items such as flags and band regalia of the field armies. (FSHM.)

In 1991, the command corridor along the second story of the Quadrangle was carpeted. A display of the flags of the states in the Fifth Army area was installed, and historical displays made by the Fort Sam Houston Museum and the Training Aids Branch were placed along the right-hand side of the corridor. (FSHM.)

Even before the attacks on the World Trade Center and Pentagon on September 11, 2001, security measures such as this fence had been installed at the Quadrangle. The stone columns between the steel fence sections replicate the existing stone columns of the entrance to the post and soften the visual impact of the fence on the historical scene. (FSHM.)

A high-security door with a keypad lock controls entry into the telecommunications center in the Quadrangle. Inside this door, a guard checks a visitor's identification card against an access roster to verify his or her eligibility to enter through another locked door. If everything checks out, the guard will buzz the visitor in. (FSHM.)

This is the view from the former USAA building toward the sally port. When the security fence went up around Fort Sam Houston, the headquarters elements across the street from the Quadrangle were isolated. To facilitate staff members going back and forth, a pedestrian gate was set up with a police officer checking credentials. (FSHM.)

Replacing the wood siding along the arcade with double-pane insulated glass restored the original appearance of the arcade while accommodating the air-conditioning. Sections of the original railing were found under the wood siding, allowing a full replication. The displays and flags along the arcade were now visible from the courtyard. (FSHM.)

Five

THE QUADRANGLE IN THE 21ST CENTURY

It was said that the world changed after the terrorist attacks on the World Trade Center and the Pentagon in 2001. The world around the Quadrangle certainly changed, as security measures increased. The entrance to the post on New Braunfels Avenue next was closed. Some of the changes were familiar—calling troops to active duty and deploying them at first to key points in the United States, then overseas to the Middle East. San Antonians who had taken for granted their ease of access to Fort Sam Houston and the Quadrangle were now cut off from "their" Army post.

In response to the Global War on Terrorism, the Department of Defense changed the mission of the Fifth Army in the Quadrangle. In 2005, the Fifth Army became the land component command for the US Northern Command, or Army North, for short. It was responsible for the land defense of the United States, including chemical, biological, radiological, nuclear, and explosive incidents and natural disaster response. Next came the creation of Joint Base San Antonio under Air Force command and the influx of some 14,000 military and civilian personnel to Fort Sam Houston.

The biggest physical change for the Quadrangle came in 2012 when Lt. Gen. Perry Wiggins decided to move the Fort Sam Houston Museum into the Quadrangle. This move had been contemplated as early as 1964 by Maj. Gen. William A. Harris, deputy commander of the Fourth Army and commander of Fort Sam Houston, who included this move in a long-range plan. General Harris had a keen sense of history. His mother had introduced a certain Lt. Dwight Eisenhower to Mamie Doud at Fort Sam Houston in 1915. Moving the museum required the relocation of the Army North staff out of the eastern wing of the building. The museum, then located on the Artillery Post, closed its doors and began to pack up its more than 10,000 artifacts. On June 8, 2015, the museum reopened to visitors. Since then, security measures have changed, and visitors can visit the Quadrangle without too much trouble.

Ft. Sam Houston, Texas

With the growing popularity of digital cameras, cell phones, and electronic means such as e-mail and social media to share images, postcards are going the way of the dodo bird, at least as far as Quadrangle postcards. A diligent search of post exchanges, souvenir shops in San Antonio, ephemera shows, and the Internet over the last five years turned up only one new card, probably from 2001. (FSHM.)

In this 2008 aerial view of the Quadrangle and vicinity, all the intrusive structures built inside the Quadrangle are gone, returning the courtyard to its earlier parklike appearance. Also gone are all the warehouses of the new depot area. Only the administrative building across the street (at far right) survives. (FSHM.)

In the main conference room, Lt. Gen. Perry Wiggins (far left) conducts a briefing for the Army chief of staff, Gen. Ray Odierno (second from the left). The oil painting in the background was created by Elias San Miguel, who had been the exhibits specialist at the Fort Sam Houston Museum. (US Army photograph.)

This view of the sign at the sally port on October 10, 2017, reads that Lt. Gen. Jeffrey S. Buchanan is the commanding general of Army North. At that time, General Buchanan was coordinating the military support during the Hurricane Irma relief operations in Puerto Rico. (Photograph by author.)

On the east wall inside the sally port are three bronze plaques. At left is a list of the commanders of the San Antonio Arsenal. At center is a copy of the tablet below the clock on the tower. *Quartermaster* is spelled correctly, however (see page 34). At right is the Gettysburg Address plaque. (Photograph by author.)

In the stairwell, this painting, *A Heritage of Service*, by Elias San Miguel and Richard Sanchez, symbolizes all who served at Fort Sam Houston. Depicted are, from left to right, Maj. Gen. John Wool, Sgt. Benjamin Bowen, Capt. John Bullis, Col. Teddy Roosevelt, Brig. Gen. John Pershing, Lt. Dwight Eisenhower, Brig. Gen. Beaumont Buck, Col. Kenichi Uchida, M.Sgt. Travis Watkins, Pfc. Edith Lipsey, Pvt. Porfilio Salinas, and Maj. W.C. Garrison. (Photograph by author.)

At this writing, the command corridor along the second story of the Quadrangle has the flags of the states displayed on the outer wall's insulated-glass outer wall. Mounted on the blocked doorways are panels depicting the history of the Quadrangle, including its animals, the military hardware displayed there, and the story of Geronimo. (Photograph by author.)

Adam Quintero has been taking care of the Quadrangle animals since 1970. An Air Force veteran and former lab technician at Brooke Army Medical Center, Quintero provides daily routine care for the animals and can call on the post veterinarian for serious problems. His office is the former Signal Corps shop on the north wall of the Quadrangle. (Photograph by author.)

The old rectangular pond was a casualty of water conservation. It leaked badly and was replaced by a more natural-looking, irregularly shaped pool with flowing water. Migrating birds often join the resident fowl at the pool. Seen here from the tower, the pond was stocked with fish. (Photograph by author.)

As it has done since it was completed in 1877, the tower looks down on the landscaped courtyard of the Quadrangle as the deer graze and the fowl forage. Meanwhile, inside the offices and unseen by visitors, the officers, enlisted personnel, and civilian employees of Army North carry out their mission like their predecessors before them. (Photograph by author.)

The Fort Sam Houston Museum opened its doors to visitors on June 8, 2015. It presents the history of the installation from its origins in 1845 as the Post at San Antonio up to the present. The different roles and missions of this installation are featured. The museum occupies almost the entire east wing. (Photograph by author.)

The museum lobby serves as an introduction to all things military for nonmilitary visitors. This room retained many of the original storeroom features to remind visitors of the original purpose of the Quadrangle. Above the front desk is Porfirio Salinas's painting of the Alamo, done in 1944 while he was a soldier at Fort Sam Houston. The doorway leads to the staff offices and collections. (Photograph by author.)

This resin bust of Gen. Sam Houston, namesake of the installation per General Order No. 99 in 1890, was made by Don R. Schol, an Army artist stationed at Fort Sam Houston in 1969. In the background, the wall retains the original appearance of the storeroom walls. The exterior walls were furred out and insulated to facilitate climate control for the protection of the collections. (Photograph by author.)

In the lobby, this is the original concrete floor. The pattern is from the tile that covered the office floor. Doorways like this one connected the offices, making it possible to traverse this wing from end to end. The path is 300 feet long as the crow flies, but much longer as it snakes through almost 9,000 square feet of exhibits. (Photograph by author.)

These two introductory panels explain the terminology of forts, posts, camps, and bases and how the terminology reflects the purpose of an installation. It also identifies the names of the historic neighborhoods at Fort Sam Houston. On the opposite side of this wall is a three-dimensional terrain model of the installation. (Photograph by author.)

This security door used to lead into the areas where classified activities were conducted by the Fifth Army. The museum retained the door as another reminder of the building's past. It now leads into the exhibit galleries. This door is secured in the open position when the museum has visitors. (Photograph by author.)

This museum presents the history of Fort Sam Houston as an example of the missions and functions of an Army installation. Six spacious former storerooms allow the display of the uniforms, insignia, weaponry, and equipment used by soldiers serving on the post over its 173-year history. (Photograph by author.)

This exhibit, entitled *Lock, Stock, and Barrel*, shows the development of the firearms used by the Army, starting with the flintlock muzzleloaders, in use from the time the Post at San Antonio was established up to the early cartridge and magazine-fed breechloaders. Another exhibit on the tour follows the development up to the present. (Photograph by author.)

This M1 75-millimeter pack howitzer was partially disassembled before it was placed into this exhibit. Early concepts of airborne operations were developed under the aegis of the headquarters in the Quadrangle. The display beyond the howitzer depicts the halcyon days of garrison life in the 1930s. The boots on the mannequin belonged to then brigadier general Dwight Eisenhower. (Photograph by author.)

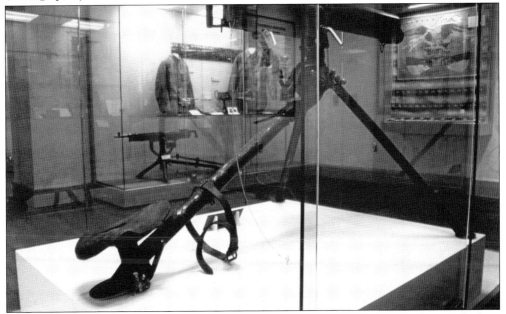

How does one keep school-aged children occupied when they visit the museum? One sends them on a scavenger hunt to find military figures, toy soldiers as it were, hiding in the exhibits. If the scavengers find them, there is a reward. Here, a machine gun crew takes cover under the rear leg of the tripod of an M1904 Colt-Maxim machine gun. (Photograph by author.)

This part of the museum is seldom seen by visitors. In this room are the staff, the reference library, and the archival collections. Through the doorway in the background are two storage rooms for the artifact collections. The first of these was the office of Col. Billy Mitchell in 1925. (Photograph by author.)

Marines from the 3rd Assault Amphibian Battalion from Camp Pendleton, California, prepare to parade the colors in the Quadrangle. Marine Corps veteran Cpl. Randy D. Mann was awarded the Navy and Marine Corps Medal during this ceremony for his actions while serving with the 3rd Assault Amphibian Battalion in 2013. (DVIDS.)

Six

HOW TO DATE THE QUADRANGLE IMAGES

The dates of Quadrangle images can usually be approximated by the buildings and features in the image. For example, if there is no clock on the tower, the image was taken between 1877 and 1882. If the clock has a dark face, the image dates between 1882 and 1907. If the clock has a light-color face, the image dates after the installation of the 1907 clock. Other features in the Quadrangle, such as the water tanks, can give clues to the dates. *The Quadrangle: Hub of Military Activity in Texas*, prepared by the Fort Sam Houston Museum in 2009, has site plans and a table listing the construction and demolition dates of most of the structures in and around the Quadrangle. By comparing the features in the photograph with those on the site plans and the table, a fairly good time frame can often be determined. This monograph is available at the library at Fort Sam Houston and in several libraries in the San Antonio area.

Postcard collectors can look at a postcard and give a range of dates based on the format used on the back of the card and the technical process used to print the image on the front side of the card. Some collectors even know the publishers' dates in business. Postmarks can be helpful but beware "the perils of postmarks." Postmarks only tell that the image was taken before that date, not when it was taken.

Sometimes, the originator of the photograph writes the date on the back. Carl Ekmark, post photographer from about 1935 to 1947, occasionally included the date of the event in the caption of his photographs. He also serially numbered his images, but using this number is not foolproof because the photographs were not necessarily numbered in the order they were taken. Ekmark would occasionally reissue an image using a different number. Sometimes, the image would be cropped differently, sometimes not.

Dating an image is not rocket science. It only takes a little knowledge and some detective work.

The clock is a key feature in dating Quadrangle images. The 1882 clock (above) had a black disc face attached to the tower at the level of the windows above the inscribed tablet, with white Roman numerals and hands. A set of the original 1882 hands is in the collection of the Fort Sam Houston Museum. The faces of the 1907 clock were recessed into the surface of the tower, with a stone border surrounding them. The faces were also slightly smaller than the originals and made of translucent white glass, illuminated from the inside at night. They had black Roman numerals and hands. (Both, FSHM.)

DEER PARK, FORT SAM HOUSTON,
SAN ANTONIO, TEXAS.

Using postmarks to date images can be deceiving. This postcard, *Deer Park, Fort Sam Houston*, is postmarked 1908 but the clock in the tower is the original 1882 clock, not the 1907 clock. The image shows the 1900 tank at far left. These two features date this image as taken between 1900 and 1907, not in 1908. (FSHM.)

The Tower, Ft. Sam Houston, San Antonio, Texas.

The presence or absence of water tanks can be useful in dating Quadrangle images. The tank at far left was erected in 1900 and removed in 1914. The tank at far right went up in 1904. The center tank was built in 1911. The last two were removed in 1984. Based on these dates, this image would have been created between 1911 and 1914. (FSHM.)

The water tanks have features other than their locations to tell them apart. The water tank at left was erected by the Virginia Bridge and Iron Company of Roanoke, Virginia. Post Engineer records states it was constructed in 1903, but the data plate attached to the structure by the builder reads 1904. The data plate is in the collections of the Fort Sam Houston Museum. The other water tank, below, added in 1911 west of the 1904 tank, can be differentiated from the 1904 by the narrower spread of the support legs. It also has bolsters around the lower edge of the tank. (Both, FSHM.)

68: — THE QUADRANGLE, FORT SAM HOUSTON, SAN ANTONIO, TEXAS

Here is another example of the perils of postmarks. The card above, postmarked 1948, seems to be appropriate for that year but the information printed on the reverse side, seen below, by the publisher mentions the VIII Corps Area and the 2nd Division. But the VIII Corps Area and the 2nd Division had been reorganized in 1942 into the VIII Service Command and the 2nd Infantry Division, respectively. The VIII Service Command moved to Dallas in December 1942. The 2nd Infantry Division left for Fort McCoy in Wisconsin in November 1942. This postcard was printed in 1942 or earlier but not mailed until 1948. (Both, FSHM.)

The key features in this postcard of the Quadrangle plaza are the water tank, built in 1900, and the original 1882 clock. These features date this image to between 1900 and 1907. The 1908 postmark on the card supports this date estimate. (FSHM.)

With the Vidales sundial and the Gettysburg Address plaque behind him, this soldier stands ready to direct traffic in the Quadrangle. A whistle hangs from his left breast pocket. The license plate on the car at right is in the colors and format used in 1935. (FSHM.)

A military police
unit, identifiable
as such by the
Sam Browne belts
and MP brassards,
passes in review
during a ceremony
in the Quadrangle
honoring Lt. Gen.
John P. Lucas,
Fourth Army
commanding
general. The
photographer,
Carl Ekmark,
has conveniently
inserted the date
of the event, "17
June 1946," into the
caption. (FSHM.)

The identification of military units in the Quadrangle gives clues to the date of the image. If the shield over the sally port reads "Eighth Corps Area," the date is between 1921 and 1941. "Fourth Army" gives a date between 1944 and 1956. "Fourth US Army" signifies 1956 to 1971. "Fifth US Army," as shown here, refers to dates between 1971 and 2005. After that, it should be "United States Army North, Fifth Army." (FSHM.)

Uniforms, insignia, or equipment used by soldiers can sometimes help date photographs. These two soldiers, "goldbricking," or goofing off, on a bench in the Quadrangle, wear uniforms typical of the First World War. But they are also wearing prewar canvas leggings, making the date of the image less certain. (FSHM.)

To the left of the sally port, the Fifth Army set up a sign with the names of the current commanding general and command sergeant major. Referring to *The Quadrangle: Hub of Military Activity in Texas* or making a quick Internet search will reveal that Lt. Gen. Freddy E. McFarren, whose name is on the sign, was commander from 2000 to 2003. (FSHM.)

ABOUT THE ORGANIZATION

Preservation Fort Sam Houston, Incorporated, a 501(c)(3) private, nonprofit educational organization not affiliated with the Department of Defense, was established in 1984 to promote and support historic preservation at Joint Base San Antonio, Fort Sam Houston and to support the activities of the Fort Sam Houston Museum. The organization participates with Fort Sam Houston in the preservation process as an interested party in the local community. It has pioneered the concept of the public-private partnership for preservation projects on military installations. The organization renovated the historic Stilwell House for use as a venue for community events at Fort Sam Houston. By 1998, the building had been restored to its previous Victorian grandeur and Preservation Fort Sam Houston held a grand reopening of the Stilwell House. In 2013, the organization nominated Fort Sam Houston for a Richard H. Driehaus Preservation Award from the National Trust for Historic Preservation, recognizing Fort Sam Houston for its partnership in federal preservation. The award was presented on November 1, 2013. When Fort Sam Houston became part of Joint Base San Antonio, the organization expanded its horizon to the historic buildings on all of San Antonio's military bases. Today, Preservation Fort Sam Houston continues its historic preservation efforts and support for the Fort Sam Houston Museum.

DISCOVER THOUSANDS OF LOCAL HISTORY BOOKS FEATURING MILLIONS OF VINTAGE IMAGES

Arcadia Publishing, the leading local history publisher in the United States, is committed to making history accessible and meaningful through publishing books that celebrate and preserve the heritage of America's people and places.

Find more books like this at
www.arcadiapublishing.com

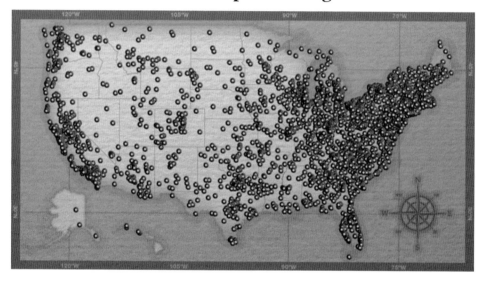

Search for your hometown history, your old stomping grounds, and even your favorite sports team.